Dance of the Kangaroos

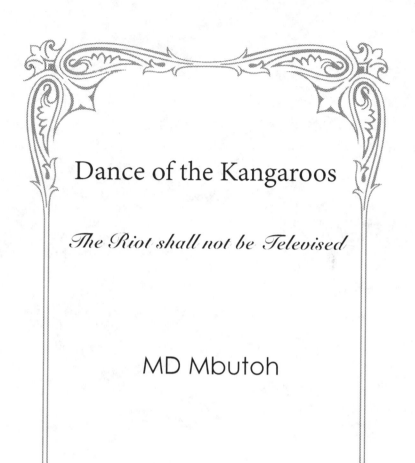

Dance of the Kangaroos

The Riot shall not be Televised

MD Mbutoh

SPEARS
MEDIA PRESS

DENVER

SPEARS MEDIA PRESS LLC

Denver

7830 W. Alameda Ave, Suite 103-247 Denver, CO 80226

United States of America

First Published in 2018 by Spears Media Press
www.spearsmedia.com
info@spearsmedia.com
Information on this title: www.spearsmedia.com/dance-of-kangaroos

ISBN: 978-1-942876-22-9 (Paperback)

Also Available in Kindle (ebook)

Spears Media Press has no responsibility for the persistence or accuracy of urls for external or third-party internet websites referred to in this publication, and does not guarantee that any content on such websites is, or will remain, accurate or appropriate.

Book Design by Spears Media Press
Cover Photograph: (CCO) Pexels.com

To all the minority groups and ethnicities around the world whose voices have been submerged by far-rights movements, hatred, racism, dictatorial regimes, war, and terrorism.
"Unto the upright there ariseth
light in the darkness: he is gracious
and full of compassion, and righteous."
—Psalms 112:4

Contents

FOREWORD

Dance of the Kangaroos (The Riot shall not be Televised) is a glaring demonstration of artistic magnanimity through which an emerging Cameroonian poet of our time unveils thick dirty layers of injustice, marginalization, press censorship, wire blockade, and a brutal response in a West African fictitious state of Kangaroo. After the publication of his first master piece *The Refugee Republic*, here comes a dazzling piece of art which the reader must afford to read.

The richness of the poems reflects the poet's patience and refined craftsmanship to excavate the ideas fully in order to enable the reader savour not just the peculiarity and uniqueness in language use, but the burden of a sadden heart. The poet penetrates the private and public spaces of a crooked regime and crooked men to reveal the whole 'truth- and nothing but the truth' of a dire situation of a once united people whose colonial past has torn them in shreds. Some of the breaking threads are marginalisation, linguistic differences, diverse and biased colonial and African cultural heritage. These broken threads have formed heavy 'walls of agony' the way Ngong Kum Ngong calls it, between the two peoples with two colonial pasts. Any attempt to break these walls of agony meets with reprisal and in order to make sure it does not attract public attention, the system makes sure "the strike shall not be televised." The regime in place, mostly constituted by some who continue to believe that for the sake of the pre-World War I umbilical cord the people shared, they should live under the same roof after being separated for almost half a century.

Mbutoh's poetry hurls you into one of the ruthless regimes in Africa that you can ever think of with all its repressive machinations. As you read along, the glow from the poems fills you with vivid, authentic, and fascinating details about the merciless treatment of the people in such a way that you find yourself suffocating within stone walls of incarceration. It is a plight that the world cannot afford to ignore, because "the strike shall not be wired" as soon as the 'crack' which has been unskilfully undermined for half a century escalates to a full-scale protest. The poems embrace and reveal the excruciating experiences of the English-speaking population of the great Kangaroo nation. While defending the due rights of the marginalized people through arts (poetry) as enshrined in the Universal Declaration of Human Rights by the United Nations, which the regime has ostentatiously confiscated, the poet meanders with tact into the intricacy of the delicate issues at stake. He further slams the regime's rigid method and diabolic approach of taking the position of the most powerful with regard to the delicate nature of the situation. The act of dictate, sobriquet, the use of brute force and the heinous actions of the military vis-a-vis the population are condemned in all its forms.

Even though united for half a century, the poet is able to infiltrate into the deep neglected wounds and increasing gaps that have existed between this 'family', which many people are unaware of because it concerns the political, economic and socio-cultural frustration of the minority. These problems had been neglected with the famous nonchalant "vous allez faire quoi" phrase and now 'light has caught us with our pants down'. To lighten things up, he pays tribute to some outstanding poets of his admiration like Wilfred Owen, Lord Byron, Mbella Sonne Dipoko, and Christopher Okigbo.

Mohammed Kiere,
African Literature Scholar, University of Yaounde I
International Relations Institute, Cameroon (IRIC)

Dance of The Kangaroos

Crack

Crack this belly and extricate the foetus,
Crack this clay pot and exhume the foetus,
Crack this egg and drop the foetus,
Did you hear that crack crack crack, brother?

Crack this code; shred the cables like venomous whips,
Shred the cords like broomsticks,
Gyrate them like the pitiless blades of the chopper,
Grrrtt! Grrrrtt! Grrrtt! Grrrtt! Grrrtt! Grrrtt!

Swirl the shredded cords like manes,
Knot the sly stripes into golden nooses
Fit for the necks of disgruntled siblings,
The extremists of reason, the dregs of
Assimilated civilization!

Crack crack crack, let's fag pot
Let's sodomise the derrières of strangers,
Pull them like the unfortunate victim of the
Knacker, cracked bones, cracked skulls till comfort
Quenches the thirst of budding freedom.

Fear not sergeant, it shall not be wired!

The Strike shall not be Televised I

Go home brothers,
Lap under the loins of your mothers,
Nap in the laps of your wives,
Feel the caressing innocence of your children,
'cos the strike shall not be wired.

There is a long ladder at the border,
A tall ladder of villainy pulling down
Freedom like a howling storm over mutating ground,
Unveiling skirts and mutilating the doors to womanhood,
No palm bird to chirp sad notes; so the strike shall not be wired.

There is a ladder at the border, shielding the wires,
Pulling off the roots of freedom and skinning its barks
Chopping off its limbs like some monstrous
Al Capone killing of Commercial Avenue—
Borrowing in muddy bathtubs in Beau—
                    these extremists of freedom!

The strike shall not be wired,
Hasten home into the gutters of
Gendarmerie bullets…   beware of farting riffles!
Did you hear that? Hell ho!
The strike shall not be wired— the long
Ladder is nibbling the wires like iron rats.

Did you say dialogue?
With kilo tons of tapes on these quavering lips?
Who will wear the wigs for me?
You sit on the cushion to dialogue,
Here I am on the laps of some sodomite— and you say dialogue?
Shouldn't dialogue be a tennis court?
Surely it shall not be wired?

Weep not, Mother

Large flare nostrils like furnaces,
Dark cold eyelids over large white pupils
Coat of red paint coats African lips like
Thick layers of camwood ov'r a virgin...
Weep not mother!
Martyrs are those who depart with heroic
Lances in brave hands.

Weep not woman,
This is the cause for which pilgrims are meant
For— pilgrims?
Smeared soles, decked in pillars of miseries;
Casting ancestral tongues, casting mothers off,
Breaking umbilical... weep not mother,

For the umbilical is alive like a young shoot
Interred in the middle of the hearth
To warm raffia wine for the elders.
Flames of self-annihilation burn within
The oppressor— weep not mother, jiggers
Can't live forever.

They have sizzled their own umbilical,
They have severed the bridge across two
Worlds and leaden the sinews of cohesion.
Dear mother, weep not for the elders
Are in battle. They have drunk from the
Calabash of innocence spilled in the hearth,
And tasted youthful tubers of green experience.

Boko Boys

They are the boko boys,
And they are the Bee Boys,
The killing field bustles with fruitfulness,
And the determination of harvesters spurs them.

Where the feet root themselves,
The eyes crow to the tunes of the mouth.
Skirmishes are blind ambiguous beasts—
A swine devouring its own placenta like
The foolish Bangolan man that mowed
His arm for an abscess-infested finger!

Boko Boys
Sweep the streets of Com. Av. with foliage of peace—
They brandish *keng* in the face of Bee Boys in Beau,
But are the eyes folded too if the heart is in coma?
They are the Boko Boys, says the cockerel's headsman
And they are the Bee Men poised for Salvation
Of legal Tyranny— Why?
'cause it won't be televised!

Foolish

Intelligent fool,
These spiteful kangaroos, springing fifteen
Metres overhead tortoises like loose bullets.
Can't you see sir, that the fiery earth cannot
Mate with the angry clouds?

They clamp cockroaches in vile civility
And tie them at the goalpost for amusement,
Foolish you of the seventh heaven, can't you see
Moles were meant to scurry the forest at night?

Loopy elders,
Distilling fine raffia with water from the Sanaga
Stream— can't you see the grimaces on the wise
Skulls of the visitors?

Wise elders,
Corking palm oil in dark brown magic calabash
In royalty's name— why put the cockerel's
Cap of leadership on a vagabond's head?

Hail elders of this vile age of restless woes,
Boats of palm oil are good in cold waters,
But your wisdom loses lustre—
For water and oil cannot mate!
Fear not champions of cowardice,
For your disenchantment won't be wired!

Scapegoats

Sleep well my love,
Doze coyly sweetheart,
I am the bald head that have borne the anger
Of incompetency,
My moral is the unbending iroko tree,
My cause resolute like the parallel races
Round the waist of the globe.

They want my head on a sinful platter;
They say I am the baptizer
And so must make an appeasement dish with my
head on a golden saucer of sin on a fiendish festivity,

Sleep well my love,
For I may not come home tonight,
I've decided to walk with the elders into
The quiet womb of the night,

The caresses of the night is balmy,
The whisper of the wind is sweet,
And the melody of the insect is divine.
The elders have pruned me into a straight baobab;
Pardon me sweetheart, if my woes won't be televised.

They say exile is the push of collective failure,
They say exile is the shame of the king,
It is wrought round his cockerel's cap of dominance
Like mating snakes under a dead palm.

So let me walk the street tonight
And drink more from the river of ancestral wisdom.

The night bird is my companion— he coos into my
Ears and feeds me things only those without comfort
Would ever eat— nights, it says, are the mirrors of scapegoats!

The Riot shall not be Televised II

Thought of penning some lucid
Verse with the churning header—
But then, who'll peruse it since the
Strike shan't be televised?

Fidgeting children, tussling furtively
Beneath grandpa's aged hammock—
Like the mole, mammoth at the verge
Of extinction, weary not for the
Skirmishes shan't be televised and the
Carcasses shan't be wired.

Sudan is bubbling with maggot
Of Civil Strife—
Violence hasn't got manhood brother,
But it impregnates with years of misery!
Even if the strike shall be televised,
The audience shan't

Smell the sickening fart
In the air,
Too pungent for indifference—
The strike shan't be televised and the
Taped mouths of the Carcasses shan't be wired.

Valley to Ngola

There is this deep trench restraining Kama from Ngola,
Deeper than the tunnel into the entrails of Ngola
This infested wound in this heroic torso of stoicism,
'Your dialect sir is incomprehensible -'
They would tell you over the valley.

Wherefore will I not feel this shit in me?
Where is my home if you tell me I am your serf?
This valley to Ngola has smitten ancestral skull
With contours of wrinkles to our existence,
Where shall the ghosts of 1/10 rest their heads?

We were at the House of the World together,
We clasped mature hands after the 1/10 Ballot,
Why should you throw a large tape on this cracked—
Massively chiselled lips of Nkalang's child?
This valley to Ngola got the maddening disease.

A rat is bleeding profusely,
A snarl is clamping its head,
A large tape is leaden upon its mouth,
A snarl is smothering its neck like soaking
Monsoon rain—
This valley to Ngola where the tall returns-
The tall of the BBs came back,
The General's too, came back-
What of the venerated Asonganyi?

Incestuous Drama

I won't cry!
After all, you're my big brother.
But please is your drama not incestuous?
Milk your bitter fruit into this immature mortar,
Yes brother squeeze your wed loin into the
Mortar of your step sister's–
father shall be proud of you!

Dip deep your masculine whisk into the
Feminine bowl of your step sister,
mother can't scold you!
Don't look at the fiery misery jumping
in and out of her forlorn pupils,
She's contented being ravished!
After all, *elle ne peut rien faire!*[1]

Play the macho with your step,
Let her bleed your contentment into her tears,
Ravish this land with the cackles of your AKs
We have decided to watch your incestuous
Drama with tapes on sour lips and bitter spittle.

You cast a monstrous spectre on history–
Aha, assimilation got no room for history!
A kite's got ominous eye for the chick;
Pardon me brother for whatever wrong I did,
Pardon me if I ain't enjoying your incestuous drama
Anymore!

This Village

History books are inked with
Sheep droppings—punctuated by liberals,
Confined to the post by anvil conformists.
Tyrants ink story books with the masses' blood,
And colour bios with beaded sweat of the commons.

The mysticism of Greed,
The hydra corruption of bad seed,
The raw cocoyam itches of bribery,
The oil and water separation of the people,
These queer legacies of greed padlock a people's luck
These self-centred head boys and girls are
The wedlock of the people.

This land is a great ancient baobab,
With maggot elders for roots,
This village, its beauty some say lies in its
Rich green turfs,
But these maggots appreciate the stench in
Its dungs… no news! After all,
it isn't the nature of maggots
To survive out of excrement?
The elders of this village,
Predatory husbands defiling
Helplessly the wife that gives them life.

Should I, or Not

I've talked of leaving, you know.
A fibre bag, a walking stick, a cap of cowries,
An elephant-stock cap of a *Bororo* man—
But I couldn't desert my village for the wilderness.
If they say history is written with blood,
Is there no history with a smile?
I ain't leaving no more.

This is my baobab though infested with maggots,
This is my potato, though infested with blight,
This is the hill where I must hunt though schooled
With ticks,
My erstwhile concubine,
Have you seen my *chinda*, please?

I hear there is a meeting in the palace today,
Do you want to weed this infested farm?
Can I have a say too in that meeting?
Oh, you say my voice ain't count much!
Even if the history of this village was inked
With our sanguinary spill?
You say it's a new form of rule queer to you?

Light has caught us

Light has caught us
With our pants down;
No time to blink!

Have you seen this *ndong*?
This is where the tornado
blew an angry pebble.
This biscuit bone—
This is the testimony of
The brotherly ravishment.

Light has caught us with hands in the basket,
Rummaging the testicles of the infants,
Coarse villain fingers over immature breasts
Like a cock over a chick!

Light has caught us
With the ancestral pipe in the mouth,
Spewing sour ashes in the face of the
World like a masquerade follower;
Shall we play the unconcerned hosts
Or we shall spew the infernal coal?

Hymn to Christopher Okigbo

What did Okigbo cross the river for?
This hymn is for the wisest of bards
Consumed by nationalist flames,
Stung by the blind tongue of justice—
Justice drunken with politics.
Politics spurred by individualism,
Individualism propped by greed,
Greed gnawed by hunger,
Hunger, grown on a mount of
Joblessness
The news slapped the children in the face,
Shook the concretised beliefs of diehards;
Have you heard, brother?
Okigbo is slain—
No!
Okigbo wandered off into the forbidden shrine
Of the gods.
He's become one of them,
For no one entered the shrine twice
It's a no exit entry, good people.
The gods are just, even to
The most beautiful stem in their backyard.

Byronic Bite

Wherefore will ye be slain in Greece?
Wasn't your umbilical interred in the
Richest of Rupert Brook's grounds
Of Great Britain?

You're the Machiavelli of loosening
Top,
Wheeling and swirling like shredded bullet
Coughed off the hot dragonic
Belly of Assimilated cannon…

We have lost touch with each other,
The picot line pulled us apart like
Feminine legs and ravished the
Womb of a dejected lady with
Mutilated Beauty.

This Byronic bite is the flame
Of marginalisation, injustice,
Battling twice like an ensnarled game
To prove your worth in a maze
Of linguistic follies.

Shall I cross the Mongolo like Byron
Sauntered the Thames?
Let me in brother!
We're drifting like the great Pangaea
And the Picot heat is altering our
Temperaments like aging green fruits.

For Sonne Dipoko

You fed from the English bowl,
Drank from the *graffi* cup,
Aped the Bakossi gourmet
Laughed the Biafra laugh,
And even dosed in Yoruba arms, some say.

Brothers across the Mongolo say you were
A sell-out
'cos you didn't pen in the assimilated
Tongue.
Did you feel the pangs of this hurt?
They took a vow;
The eastern wind shall blow over the
Queen's offspring!

—*Et vous aller faire quoi?*[2]
They tell us!

I

Hands Up for the
Guns to belch!
And the guns belched.
Just at the time when friendly hands
Were to clasp each other, the guns
Vomited their venoms on naked
Populace.

Mountains of arsenals,
Smitten on grunting pickups, walled with
Human props, muscled by iron sinews,
Poised to char human earth for sport;
Down with Extremists!
So the guns vomited
And the people had a hot bath.

II

Hands Up for the
Guns to belch!
The guns belched ggg-r-r-r-r-r-r-r-r-r-r-r-r!
Just in time when friendly hands
Were to clasp each other, the guns
Vomited their venoms onto the naked
Populace:
pow-pow-pow-pow-pow-pow-pow-pow!
Then smoky silence.

!
2nd
Mounts
Of chilly arsenals,
Smitten on pickups, walled with
Bugled bodies, muscled by metal sinews;
And
Down with
Extremists!
So the guns regurgitated
And the people drank the vomit
Of the monstrosity— its funeral pyres
Augmenting, like dropping coal.

The Good Faith

This wind comes in good faith, I tell us,
This wind of good faith, coming to us,
Coming in with a bemused face— this wind
Of good fate— riding on a stallion's hide...

The eastern wind of good faith is here, almost
But lo it's here!
Ribs cackling in the harmattan tornado,
Plucking heads from fresh stems
Like cotton wool

Seasoning disgruntled minds with
Mercury pepper,
Are those human skulls?
No sir!
We come in good faith, no scuffle
To be-ruffled the wings of the hawk.

Is there a problem?

I grasped the winds,
I question the wind,
That sails across all locked cracks,
Grasping it in its locks, feeling its
Spiky strands,
gleaming in the forks
Of callous blacksmith's fingers
Is there a problem?
Stealthily it whistled in my calm ear,
Is there a problem?

Pieces of Molière's tongues
Breaking your ear like broken clay,
Gapping into contorted faces.
They ask you if you got a patois,
And you say yes— then cackling
Beagles of gestating French hens,
Spewing stupidity like wood ash!

Your YES is a problem,
And your NO would mean
Steel in their nepotistic teeth,
And the cool wind balms the
Linguistic cracks under the
 pores of breathing patois.

Post of Command

Pieces of notes before you,
Staring into dilating pupils,
Squinting like some vile viper.

Dancing fickle light of French words
Against overworked face of graffi,
Sockets like gigantic pores driven into rocks,
Dilating pupils like shaky frightful bulbs,

With revolting sinews they fling furnace in
alternation infernal tongues like confuse hails.
Then the boss, a possible dropout,
Dropout in ranks and grades,
Bossy in position,
Barks the German shepherd
Style—
A votre service, patron![3]
Like thunderous voice of
A running stomach…

Pain

In English it is "pain" asshh!
In French, it is "bread" wow!
Day and night, these things!
Some garrulous fellow- a fine one
 may whistle in a "33" symphony

a web of *pain* feeds mouths on
breathing ground,
a web— a dozen ounce of pain
squeezes spring from acrid eyes
on this breathing ground,

there is a contagious fit in
our dwelling place,
cleansing ribs clean off some
assimilated powder.
A few have caught it,
That is the one thing needful
Pain cannot suit.

Di-Vide

I can't dodge from your
Accusing finger,
I can't circumvent your finger
Of justice keen at my faults,
But blunt at the rest four in reverse.

But who's got that wisdom wig
To roll my perfection unquestionable?
A trace at God's stripe,
That's the pebble that I am.
Your finger of justice induces me
More righteous than I should.

I grope like a spectre,
With furtive eyes constantly
At the watch out for some dreadful
Steps at my rear.
Your finger of justice is a di-vide
Prided by the fume in your throat
For national unity.

Can't you behold the valley the finger
Maps on the skulls of the patriarchs?
I can't in the ways of chameleons be you,
Condescend to the irrefutable fact!
You can't be me, me can't be yo'
But we could sip from a semblance
Mug of equality.

I Come in Peace

I am in gestation,
Will soon be nursing the child of
peace I'd borne for ages of torments,

I've come, not to vomit the slime
Of hatred piped in me by ages of
Nonchalance and pulsating skulls of whitewash
Civility, but to inter and host its funeral.

I have come beaten by loneliness
And crucified by careless bugling— Second Class!
This is the baby I've nursed for fifty-seven days plus
This baby is come of age and must be
Whined.

You injected this cursed child,
This cursed child of the gods must go
Back to the shrine of the gods,
they are the sagest.

Fear not brother,
Guard your peace, for the dialogue
Shall not be wired.
The dialogue and the burial shall not
Be televised!

Where were you?

Can you scent the powder?
Can you smell the smoky coal?
Can you sniff the charred earth?
The goring skulls smiling in junctions?
Skulls laugh on the storms of fresh
elephant stocks!

Should your memories fade so easily,
Hear this out:
Can you drink from a cup of vinegar?
Yes they did!
Those skulls did gulp from gallons of vinegar
In the name of fatherland and pride!
Oh yes they did, where were you?

The forebears
Sound their names in the market
Square,
Pipe their names with pride, let their
Names dance on diplomatic tables for
They paid the price, and where were you?

Their fall was your rise
Their cry was your smile
Their slavery was your freedom
Their pains your pleasure
Their charred bottoms— were you there?

Enough! Enough!
When shall civil ungratefulness die?
When shall patriotism inter neo-colonial

Nostalgia? Hope you'll be there?
Why shouldn't the strike be wired?

Where were you
On the cross of independence?
Were you on the cross of freedom?
Did you bear the white shells of angry
White big guns like baobab bottoms?
Where were you on the altar of freedom?

Night Call

This night,
The moon is in delirium;
Pupils a little ajar, squinting over a deaf city,
This is the city of power & meekness, the stage
button for the national drama.
never to be wired.

This night,
A foreboding one, a wet blanket on grumbling volcano,
Stripes of dim shadows dancing in…amid
Serrated dry harmattan foliage, dogs roar
Amid desperate bleats of midnight sheep on twos.
never to be wired.

This night
Sleeps in silent frightfulness; terrified infants
Squeal before dancing spectres of stranded
Forebears groping through this fornicating city,
Ajar sepulchres, just hours before Hamlet's ghostly call.
never to be wired.

This night,
A slumbering sow, stinking dentals,
Pungent annals guarded by scrambling flies,
Piglets brooding amid the remnants of forgotten husbands
And lonely bachelors seasoning bottles in sweating pops,
never to be wired

This night,
Looming masked voodoos chieftains dancing
Round junctions, decorating entrances

With totems of vultures- a cast of
Spiritual nets over trapped souls into the drinking
Pots of selected octogenarian *njangi*-
never to be wired.

Most Powerful

Flashy impression of a tired soul
Drawn into a faithful cushion,
Kissing the rims of a Bordeaux glass and
Having sex with cold smooth fermented wine.

A pair of blind glasses astride a badly written
M-nose, the head of an adder.
Dad, behold the most powerful man! My 5 year old
Yelps, little feet crushing a stoic cushion with mirth,

Most powerful man in this triangle,
His words, a river of life-giving brook,
A click of shy fingers blows off the candle in you,
The most powerful man in this triangle,

The most powerful?
Muscular like Super Makia?
Or stifling gloves like the Jungle Rumble hero?
Surely they shall not be televised, or wired?

His Excellency Abroad

An ulcer into the belly of an iron bird,
A forest of purple uniforms chained the eaves
Of a blood coloured carpet, extricating from
The mammoth coffin into the humming bird,
His excellency in the departure lounge.

A famish group weave a human noose
round skin drums, beating them to insanity.
Muscular fingers squeezing the vocal cords of the
Sad drums into forced merriment.

Whistles trickling into eardrums like typhoons,
Unmuting calmness from a mutiny of complaints.
Have you seen his majesty, he's got to be swallowed
Soon in the stomach of grunting iron bird— en route to
Boot-sharped Island.

The stinking shit of discontent looms in a hypocrite air,
Hedges bore the weights of dissidents poised with bows,
But wherefore are the arrows?
Leaded! The wind whistled in the grunting voice of a
Foreign iron bird.

The women shall have no sleep

In this house, they say the women shall
Not sleep - they're the curers of boredom,
One I do know from years back used to bear
Vulture's nest, especially on diplomatic walks.

She got the peculiar nest,
Her eyes bathed visages, her active eyes
Sweetening vinegar throats softening bile.
This is the house of women, the testicles of
Male cowardice and inabilities,

Have you got her the lawful way?
Hell no, the father of men shall not weep
For the girl shall not complain the stranger's trashing,
A handful of scums stifling the future's necks
With wires though the strike shan't be wired

The strike shall not be wired,
The strike shall never be televised,
It hasn't got a face, at least not now, no compatriot?
It shan't be wired for peace is a slumber and anarchy
Cropping giant steams with each round of the eastern
Traveller,

Even women shan't be televised,
They too shan't be wired at least not colluded
With carnal drunkenness of this dissidents—
She shall put a switch on iron testicles and click
Them with blinking eyelids till ye let go future's throat.

Astride the Mongolo

I can't close this 50kg of eyelids,
Ominous hands of grieve are smoothening
These beaten shoulders with tyrannical dexterity
The night's silence, a true obedient dog,
Even the infant is at peace with slumber today!

But across the Mongolo,
Deep into the intestines of this forest lies
Impending inferno of satiated patience and
Monstrous silence of a boa constrictor,

Over the river between,
I know there is a vengeful lad weeping for the
down pour of innocent blood licking rich grounds,
yet the Nation's mirror and flag say the volcano
has become a lake of snow. But I know better;
Interred beneath the calm of backbiting, the strike had
not been wired!

A cold wax of national snow dancing on the
Belly of gestating green lava,
Each cackling of legal arsenal boils the lava,
Each pull on the loin of a varsity maiden ripens this
Cold volcano to maturity yet the strike shall not be wired

We'll scurry back to our vomit with majesty
Like Rwanda 94,
This is the voice of he whom the gods cursed with
Unbelieving truth weeping on the bridge of Mongolo,

Won't you wire this dejectedness?

Keng Plant

Take this *keng* plant with a bow,
Boil it, and gulp for your identity delirium!
But I ain't got identity delirium!
But *keng* are meant for peaceful handshake!
No doubt! Yet a mirthful handshake, no his majesty?

Ummp, ummp, *mais qu'est-ce que vous voulez?*[4]
Sincerity ain't bought on the altar of keg plant,
But earned under the tree of *keng*, your highness!
Your *keng*, I've got the finest from the Grassfield,
Won't you sweeten your throat with this *sweet-alakata-pepper?*

Sorry your highness, *sweet-alakata-pepper* graces the heels
Of trouble shooters!
I ain't one then with this bag of tiger hides, keng plant, and
The finest of *sweet-alakata-pepper?* Peace your highness,
clads itself in humane hides, not three cotton pieces.

No father with grains of the loin spanks
His infant to death, your highness!
No loving father, your lordship turps upon the loin
Of his own grains of the groin, no brother tastes of
His feminine half's pot of *egusi*, the gods sail in the clouds
And the chief priest is powerless—

Go, go, go your highness!
The gods sail on the mutinying clouds,
The forebears move swiftly amid tree backs,
Can you behold the visages meddling amid the crowds?
The furious tornado is descending off the Ngoketunjia and the
Chief priest is abroad! Shall the ravages be televised, your
highness?

Repair

It takes two for a progeny, no?
This progeny is clad in kingly lining,
Shimmering with dubious smile of indifference,
But who will claim its paternal authorship?

We shall make the beast with two backs,
But a maiden can't gestate from a mangrove,
Won't you lay down your groin, comrade?
Repair for the strike that never was wired commences
With the turping of your yew with our yew

Your highness, won't you untie the goats
Tethered behind your secret huts?
They were clipped last nights and stolen across
The Mongolo, won't you say something, his lordship?
You've got to repair this dancing hut before the rains
Return from its monsoon journey.

Hands raised, bows cut, arrows broken
And we come surf on the sail of peace and oneness
On this brown harmattan sea of dust,
You've been put in the family way by wrath, but
We can't bear that pot anymore… won't you repair this too?
Oh, it shan't be televised too!

Where do we anchor?

I fear even my own steps these days
I curve the granites on snaky path, irking over
Comments from wild fowls and sly beast
I fright even the sound of my breath,

My breath scares me to the marrow,
My whoopee snows are alien to my anxious ears,
Can't you see this paranoid is taking a monstrous
Form of the tall?
My mat in the right hand, a kid on old back, a wife
In the left hand, journey of the magi is set into the
Solace of the neighbour's haven.

Shall we get a refreshing calabash from Uncle Tafawa?
Ah silly me!
I'd mocked his wisdom severally put his grey wisdom
Turf to the test—
How loopy I'd been with age old wisdom!
We'll anchor across the Manyu forest, in the womb of Enugu.

What's wrong with Y'all?

I'd brushed my throat with a bag of salt each day
for fifty years,
rolled my words on a sieve and tossed them over seven times
before gracing your impatient ears,
yet you've always found fine clippers to mutilate each word
carefully dropped onto your itching ears
won't you play the attentive master, at least for once?

What's wrong with y'all?
I ain't got a national patois, never!
Peuchop is my clan's tongue— by it I shall
Bear witness I was bred by a mother,
But English is my language, that which you play deaf to!
You think you're better with a golden snot on
A stupid nose? What's wrong with y'all? Can foolishness
Play well its own foolishness to the amusement of stupidity?

Tons of hatred lurks in your Frenchified   eyes
Like green caterpillar beneath short-lived shimmering
Leaf waiting to wither with the blinking of the sun,
Trailers of segregated remorse foam within you like
The dancing Fontem on the eternal Menchum drum -
Draining your energy like transistor and goldstone,
What's wrong with y'all?

Have we become that rotten, a national egg?
This inherited crown is the antic of a past engagement
Whose husband left, shall you punish a wife for losing
A fiancé to free will?
You had danced in our yard like the *nko'o*
Hitting your gongs frantically like a *chinda* in the *Gumba's* grove,
What's become of the enthusiastic fiancé?

Before Sunrise

Before the sun rises,
Before sunrise, I shall play the serpent
In the early warmth of burning hearth
Purring over a lion brother I lost to strangers,
Before the sunrise, oh yes before the sunrise,
I would set out for a long trek into the unknown
Like the prodigal's father to
Whence dwell my brother, my umbilical,

Before the sunrise, I will squirrel like the late
Mole into my brother's hole to harvest from his
Tree of anger the poisoned fruit that will purge
This battered bones across the sweet scented old river;

Have you seen the wise boatman?
Give him the holy hint,
Before sunset, I shall sail with him into the
Glory of wisdom and festivity for a life well spent,
But boatman, two cowries have I got from this
Loin and two have the ancestors claimed,

I've got only my brother from a similar umbilical,
Who severed our sacred charms too — but before the sunrise
I would grace his hut and chew my eternal cord.
I stand before him and by that he's got duty to
Render to the gods, if not me!

Before the sunrise,
I shall inter the dozen years of hot anger beneath this
Epiglottis and feather this old heart beneath severed torso,
Yes my kinsmen, he who is fool is he that thinks himself wise

At all moments. I ain't wise, never hath been.
So before sunrise, I would to the eyes of the eastern traveller
Tread my soles into the direction of light, for whence
Comes the steam of the sibling.

Multitask Force

A dog mistook its master for thief,
And slumber under balmy kisses of a visitor's caresses,
This multi-something streaming into my drums,
Does it wave the people's green banner or
the people's masters' to a brittle showdown?

Multilingual task force
Has waved off the roots of the baobab
As its lumbermen poise to ambush!
Did I hear these soldiers of B.M. task were
Handpicked by his majesty's goodwill?

Forget it brother,
A new song has been piped on the
Machiavelli gramophone again;
They word us dude, they word us like
The woodpecker who never a promise fulfil,

Power has given them a pinch of snuff,
And a tap on the collar gallops their cerebrums
Down a slushy hill of delicious bigotry!
Behold they ski with the drumbeats of
Greed… Terror eyes sneak through innocent hedges,
Silent indifference and passionate apathy.

Never the Same!

Yesterday we were monsters
Of others,
Today we are our own monsters;
Wrecking peace,
Raking juicy turfs,
Rigging particles of peace,
And grappling with that which never
Would succumb under our bully paws

We're our own undoing,
We have become our own monsters,
Wracking deep into the abyss of hot air
Sinking deeper into loosening peace and,

Today we have just become those things
Once repugnant to our nostrils yesterday,
Peace was here- till yesterday,
But then, nights have sly ways of materialising

Nightmares into reality,
This morning, we hate ourselves more than
Love can bear—
We have become that, which we detested yesterday,
Our eyes can only pour rivers of regrets,
For we have simply become gallons of brittle vinegar.

Cannibals

We ate that human in us
Like the sow ravishes the piglets,
We threw it down like a coarsen
Placenta,
Seasoned it with backbiting in gallons,
Salted it with jars of hatred,
And baked it like sinners in purgatory.

We ate the human in us,
Like a madman spurns jiggers from
Soaking toes and grind them a score
And dozen stones in nutrition store…
We've become cannibals of ourselves

We have eaten the human in us,
And the human in others are species
On the edge of leprous morality
That dance a prosaic lullaby on feeble leg.

Mere shadows lingering under the indifferent
Eyes of unconcerned sun,
Stepping into forbidden shrines of sanctums
Deflowered by insatiable priests putting God
In delirium!

If the Sun Could Speak! I, II

I

Have you ever imagined the sun
Could speak?
Would it tell of the mysteries of creation!
If the sun could but say a few words,
Would it tell us why continents
Lie apart like shredded limbs
Yet very closely knitted from the curvatures
At their edges!

If the sun could speak,
Would it tell us how the same blood runs
In trillions of veins who've got
Different chlorophyll and melanin?
If only the sun could speak, would it
Tell us if Hitler did leave his Bunker?

If it could speak, the sun,
Would it tell us why Alexandria lost its
Glory to Cambridge and Oxford Presses?
Would it tell us why the Pharaoh's haven
Hath become a market place whence no
Visitor comes to stay?

Imagine the beams of the sun
Caressing your African skin, a sonorous
Voice counting your ancestry on a mammoth
Screen hung on the moon's hook!
Imagine if the sun could tell us, how skins

Materialised; Pangaea falling in pebbles till
The Americas, Europe, Asia, Australia turned their
Backs on Africa!

How the earth's anger taunted the Pangaea,
Flushing its annals with torrents of Atlantic
Vomits and giant fingers of Pacific arms waging
It on the leeward till it did bow to let go!
Only if the oldest servant could speak!

II

The Americas waving across the Atlantic,
Europe bowing to the Sahara desert, Asia scrubbing
Its soles on Africa's hair, and Australia, all smiles and
Affability, raising its sandy hat over its Pacific sands!

Imagine if the sun could speak!
Would it tell us how Picot held the ruler
And Milner blotted the Line over the buttocks
Of Kamerun; tracing his incisor ball point
from Banguran's back yard across the belly of
Bangwa/Bamileke and to the Mongo?

Would it tell us if the strike was
Ever televised?
I mean, if only the most faithful source
Of power and the oldest witness of God's
Master pieces could speak;
Would it tell us if the strike was ever wired?

Visit of Boots

I am in gestation and my
Belly aches when each day is interred.
I just realised that my gestation
Augments each passing day,
My gestation,
Gestated for a cause I seem to have been
Pulled in, even when I did not ask for it.

I've been sucked into a howling tornado
At its youthful stage.
It inhales me like the astronaut's hole!
It impacts me.
No,
It impregnates me with sperms of anarchy…
With an infant of wary heads like *afo-akom*
Wherefore should I be ravished,
 even when I didn't want to?

Did I hear someone at my door!
Can it be my loved ones, come to cheer me up?
Aha! It must be my loved ones
But have I got one?
The strike that was never wired mutilated them…
Clicking them like shattering bullets in the streets
Of Azona, for that's what they'd called it.

But the strike was never televised!
The upheaval never spied in the eyes of the screen,
How can I open when angry boots howl doors
Under the scrutiny of the indifferent night?
Aha!

Boot!   Boot!   Boot!
The boots again!
Can those be friendly boots?
They had   boot!   Boot!
BOOT!
And   booted my
Seeds fallen from my groin…
and booted the stem

From whence I fell!

Come buy a brother

Brothers you would think were brothers!
In all shapes and affability,
Casting furtive predatory glances like
A jovial squirrels,
Clad in three pieces of decaying
Coloured wool.

Brothers you think are brothers,
Babbling about some best stars
Building in some faraway lands only
Them and the evil spirits of the land
Know where such crazy lands are,
These stale brothers!
Spitting pieces of yesterday's sour wine,
Eating proud words of segregations.

When you tell them their cords
Entrails are wrecking eardrums of silent
Passers-by, they give you that monstrous
Stare of a suicide note;
'Who be you, *pauvre anglo*'[5] my honest
Brothers would thunder like angry gods
Of the Thames…

These cutest brothers of ours,
Finest in wine tasting & culinary
Finest in currency accounting,
Finest at treasury confusion…
These best brothers of mine— the finest of
Brothers one won't desire!
Too bad, not very best at cracking the
Bones of disgruntled siblings.

Beaten by the Rain

A wet chicken, we have become…
Not that I care,
man yi head, na yi neck carry am[6]
We often say in this village.

But I feel so cold under this rain,
Too cold to complain,
Too feeble to wade off these harsh flashes
Of heaven's tears lashing on English flesh
Like some atonements for future sin.

This rain of coercive repentance,
I shall repent, if I the heavens could send
Me just a glimpse of the sun to reprimand
Me of the crime I am still to commit,
But this rain is killing the me in you…

Yes, this rain is killing the you in me,
And slaughtering the us in you…
Bit by bit, the bottle gets full…
But you see brother, I am pregnant with
Gallons of this rain

I am drowning in the belly of a sea
I'd never travelled on… did I travel
In my fanciful doldrums? This rain brother
Is suffocating you in me, don't you see?
The gallons of water you spew won't make you
Swim on acrid land!

Put off the tap and let's to the sunny
City of Saga bask in the beams of reconciliation.
I know the hydra's strike wasn't wired,
So I won't count heads when I clasp your friendly
Hand and swim with caution in your affable smiles.

In your sun

We have basked in your sun,
Eating every ray with silent agony
Till the store can take no more.

We have drunk from the
Gallons of your biting words to the
Brim of this earthen jar.

We are gasping under the
Sea of your cesspit and spittle
Like fishes in toxic water.

We are constipated with rotten
Pieces of decaying fresh shit;
Searing and soaking into our intestinal
Walls— wuuuuaaaa!

33

Trente-trois!
I didn't think this was incidental,
Yet the consternations smeared me
In the face like a baby put affright;
King of Jews at 33,
At the herm at 33,
Visit at 33,
Can this be incidental prance?

Consolidate at 83,
Unsettled at 93,
Changed the custom at 03,
And harness the hide in 13,
Before that, massive wealth at 35,
Wherefore arth thou with cubic figures?

Can this be incidental?
Juxtaposition with the Jewish king
Would be too high an honour,
But would you be a better monster?

We choose silence over million

Layers of Truths before us,
We chose silence in the face of adversity,
Though silence got the complacent
  voice of collusion.

I shall choose silence, for that is what the
Cow taught its calf… that's why the strike
Was never wired.
Can you call your child by names you didn't give?
Can a stranger christen your child while you
Gaze under the generosity of the sun?

We choose silence over garrulous hypocrisy,
Falsehood is palatable falsification of truth,
Falsehood is tipsy with greed when it does
Truth encounter,
No sir, we choose to bathe in a river of silence
And watch the civilised hypocrisy *juju*
Itself down the valley of destruction

We choose muteness over mirthful pains,
For this is a silence that will change everything,
This is a truth that will brittle the hoax cap of
Peace—
We shall choose silence over coarse truth,
For truth treads on straight path.

ENDNOTES

1. There is nothing she can do (French).
2. And what are you going to do about it? (French).
3. At your service, boss! (French).
4. But what do you want? (French).
5. English speaking population in Cameroon are sarcastically referred to as 'anglo' or 'anglofou'(anglo-fools).
6. A Pidgin expression which means every person for him/herself.

ABOUT THE AUTHOR

M D. Mbutoh is an award-winning poet from the North West Region of Cameroon. He holds a BA in English Language and Literature from the University of Yaoundé. He is currently pursuing a Master's in International Communication and Public Actions at the International Relations Institute Cameroon (IRIC). He has taught Literature and English Language in secondary schools in Cameroon. His literary works have appeared in journals, blogs, and newspapers across the world including *Refugee Republic* (poetry collection) 2017, and *Praxis* (2017). His debut play, *Coastland of Hope* (2016) was commended by the BBC Radio Play in 2017. He was guest writer in the **Short Story Day Africa Flow Workshop** in 2016 and 2017 respectively, as well as guest writer for the Bakwa Magazine Creative Writing Workshop in 2016.

Printed in the United States
By Bookmasters